STARTING WITH

MICE, RATS AND GERBILS

Georg Gassner

Translated by Astrid Mick
Edited by David Alderton

BLANDFORD

Contents

Introduction

Of all the mammals, rodents are probably the only group towards which people have such an ambiguous attitude. On the one hand, mice are looked upon as cute and amusing creatures while, on the other, they are regarded as pests that devour our food stores and need to be controlled. Their small, shiny, black-button eyes, soft fur and inquisitive behaviour, however, will usually convince us of their lovableness.

This book deals with three types of rodents – mice, rats and gerbils – all of which have something in common:

- They are ideal for novice pet-keepers.
- They are readily available and inexpensive to buy.
- They do not take up a great deal of space and do not need much food.
- Compared with other small pets, they are just as easy to keep but are more intelligent and inquisitive.

Zoologically speaking, the word 'mouse' is a term that embraces hundreds of small rodents but, in this book, it is used to refer strictly to the domesticated forms of the **house mouse** (*Mus musculus*), which are often sold as 'white mice' although they also occur in a wide range of colours and varieties. Rats are very closely related to mice and are grouped with them in the same subfamily. The rats referred to in this book are the domesticated relatives of the **brown rat** (*Rattus norvegicus*).

Gerbils belong to a different zoological group, being more closely related to hamsters. Generally speaking, the **Mongolian gerbil** (*Meriones unguiculatus*) is the only species widely kept as a pet.

A wild mouse sniffs the air.

Previous pages: A pair of mice peer curiously from the pocket of their owner's jeans.

Opposite: In and out, up and down! This section of a branch with holes bored in it serves these mice as a multi-storey house with passages and hiding places.

A ladder will provide your pets with exercise – and a place to sit!

Things to consider beforehand

Before acquiring a rodent as a pet, it is worth considering the following points:

- Small rodents, such as mice, rats and gerbils, do not attain a great age compared with dogs and cats. Nevertheless, before acquiring any, it is worth considering carefully whether you are prepared to look after them for the next 2–4 years (even 5 years for gerbils).
- Are you able to spend at least half an hour a day with your pets? An even greater amount of time should be spent with solitary animals because, in the absence of other members of their own species, they need human beings for companionship.
- Are you able to leave your pets in capable hands during your holidays, e.g. with friends or neighbours?
- Have you any qualms about handling and touching the rodents that you have chosen?
- Are you willing to put up with traces of gnawing, food strewn about, dust and, despite meticulous cleanliness, the smells that may arise?
- Do you have a place in your house where your pets can be kept without disturbing anyone?
- Are you or any of your family allergic to fur or dust?
- Are all members of your family agreeable to keeping these pets?

A mouse, rat or gerbil as a present?

So often we are advised that it is good for children to grow up with pets because the task of looking after another living creature helps to develop their sense of responsibility. Small rodents have certain requirements of care (see later) that can be fulfilled by young people or an older child. Lively mice are, however, probably not so suitable for children younger than 7 years old.

Generally speaking, giving a rodent as a surprise present is not a good idea, if only in the interests of the animal. Any decision about taking on the responsibility for and care of an animal should be made by the potential pet-owner him- or herself. Unfortunately, many young mice and rats still arrive unexpectedly in a household because one member of the family, unable to resist

At first glance, domesticated mice, rats and gerbils are barely distinguishable from each other but the body size (minus the tail) alone will supply more information. Far left, top: *A house mouse 7.5–9 cm (3–3 1/2 in).* Far left, bottom: *Mongolian gerbils with furry tails 11.5–13 cm (4 1/2–5 in).* Left, top and bottom: *Brown rats 20–22 cm (8–9 in). Different colour varieties of all three species are shown.*

the appeal of those bright little eyes, has been tempted into making a hasty purchase.

Is your home suitable for rodents?

Rodents can never be given too much room – only too little! **Draughts** near a window, too much **heat** from sunlight or radiators, and sources of **noise** and **tobacco smoke** should be avoided at all costs when positioning the cage or container.

Draughts and smoke will make rodents sick, while too much heat will cause them to be lethargic and may even lead to heat stroke. Being surrounded by constant bustle will cause mice and rats to become nervous and to display frantic behaviour. It goes without saying that you should not put the cage in a cool, damp room, e.g. a cellar.

The cage or container should be positioned in a slightly **raised** position because rodents react very strongly to 'danger from above' – even if it is the well-meaning and familiar hand of their owner.

The right kind of cage or container

You can choose from two basic types of accommodation:
- A glass or plastic (acrylic) container.
- A cage with bars.

An **aquarium tank**, even a leaky one, or a **vivarium**, with sliding panels at the front, which can be securely closed, and ventilation bars at the side, will serve as very practical accommodation for mice. Gerbils, which scratch and dig a great deal, should be kept only in glass or plastic tanks.

In the case of a glass tank, make sure that the height is no greater than the width. Air cannot circulate freely in a tank that is too high or too narrow and moisture will condense and create a fertile ground for the growth of harmful micro-organisms.

Ideally, the dimensions (length × width × height) of a glass tank intended for a pair of mice or gerbils should be 90 × 30 × 38 cm (36 × 12 × 15 in). For one to three rats, it should be considerably larger: about 100 × 40 × 35 cm (39 × 16 × 14 in).

Glass vivariums, which are usually intended for reptiles, have one great disadvantage in that the ventilation grids and gliders of the sliding panels are often made of plastic, which rodents find easy to gnaw. It is probably better not to keep gerbils in this type of container, compared with a glass tank, which does not provide them with the same opportunity to burrow.

Above: *A size comparison of a fully grown mouse, gerbil and rat.*

A **lid**, consisting of a wooden frame covered with wire mesh, should be fixed to the top of any aquarium tank because all these rodents are good jumpers. Make sure that wooden parts are out of reach of the rodents' teeth and that the lid fits firmly on the tank – rats, in particular, will often lift it up. You may want to weight it down carefully.

Another means of housing small rodents is a **wire cage**. In my opinion, mouse-cages in pet-stores are often far too small and do not offer the occupants enough room to move about. Rectangular birdcages with narrowly spaced bars – 6–7 mm (¼ in) for mice and 10–12 mm (½ in) for fully grown rats – may also be used but are not ideal.

Such cages usually have only a small opening for food, which is quite impractical. Other disadvantages are the drawer at the bottom, which means that urine can run into the gaps between the drawer and the floor of the cage (rodents prefer to relieve themselves in corners), and, more importantly, the fact that rats are able to open cage-doors quite easily. These should be secured with a clip if necessary.

Hamster cages are much more suitable, particularly if they have two storeys. Older rodents will be unable to squeeze through the narrow bars and the cage-door is usually large enough for the owner to reach into all corners of the cage without difficulty. Unfortunately, this type of accommodation is unsuitable for rearing litters because young animals of all these rodent species are able to slip through even the narrowest gap.

Above: *A drinking-bottle containing water attached to the outside of the cage is very popular.* Below: *This mouse-cage offers various possibilities for climbing and hiding on several levels.* Bottom left: *A drinking-bottle has been fixed to the cage.*

Mothers with young should be kept only in glass aquarium tanks. Rats can easily be kept in guinea-pig-cages which have more widely spaced bars (10 mm/¹/₂in).

Competent home-carpenters could even attempt to construct their own accommodation for rodents. Melamine-coated chipboard about 12–15 mm (¹/₂ in) thick is eminently suitable for the purpose, provided that the rodents cannot get at the edges and gnaw them.

Drinking-water is not very important for mice but a little sip now and then is still quite welcome.

Equipping the cage or container

A home for gerbils
Mongolian gerbils, which inhabit steppe regions in the wild, are used to dry conditions and must be able to dig. This should be considered when equipping their container (preferably a glass tank).

Standard **wood shavings**, as sold for animal bedding, are recommended for litter. A layer about 4–6 cm (1¹/₂–2¹/₂ in) deep will provide a very suitable substrate for the rodents to dig in, as well as being relatively free of dust; easy to vacuum up and light in weight.

Some people use fine, dry **sand**, such as that sold for the bottom of birdcages. Sand has various disadvantages as a substrate for

A decisive factor for the well-being of your pets is sensible equipment, suitably distributed in your rodents' home. You need to distinguish carefully between the needs of mice and rats and those of gerbils.

This is one way of providing exercise for your pet!

a rodent's quarters: it does not absorb moisture as well as wood shavings and, being heavier, restricts the rodent's digging activities. It is also more expensive and can be more difficult to dispose of when soiled.

Sawdust from carpentry workshops is not recommended because it is usually contaminated with varnishes, etc. and also creates far too much dust. It may also irritate the rodents' fairly prominent eyes.

Special safe **paper bedding**, also available from pet-stores, is the best option for all these rodents. A deep layer on top of the shavings will provide something in which gerbils can burrow.

Place a small glass or ceramic **dish** full of **sand** in the cage so that your gerbils can indulge in their beloved sandbaths which keep their fur in good condition. The sand should be changed every few days. It is best to leave the dish of sand in the cage for only half an hour at a time so that it will stay clean enough for several sessions.

Soil is not suitable for litter. It may conform to the aesthetic sense of many human beings – i.e. bringing a touch of the wild into the rodent home – but moist soil is likely to be harmful to gerbils and will inevitably stain their fur. In addition, soil often contains disease organisms and parasitic worms. Peat should not be used for conservation reasons and, in any case, becomes dusty when dry.

Upside-down, unglazed clay **flowerpots** or dishes, with a diameter of about 12–14 cm (5–5$^1/2$ in), have proved to be an ideal shelter. Either partly bury the pot in the litter or carefully knock out a hole about 5 × 5 cm (2 × 2 in) across at the edge of the pot to serve as a means of entry. Take care because the edges will be sharp; they should be smoothed down with a piece of sandpaper or a file.

This type of shelter is cheap, has a built-in ventilation facility (the drainage hole) and is easy to clean with hot water. These pots and dishes are also popularly used by gerbils as look-out towers. Various playthings of this type are available from pet-stores, in the form of old boots and other moulded designs.

Wooden **nesting boxes** are less suitable as shelters because they are usually gnawed to bits in a very short time. Paper tissue or hay can be used as nesting material.

If you wish to add some decoration to your pet's home, remember that gerbils inhabit open spaces and like to move around without obstacles. Dry **wood**, as sold for aquariums, looks attractive and will serve as a look-out point, as well as being something to gnaw. Stones, particularly the smooth, round ones which are easy

to clean, are less suitable because they usually do not stand very firmly, especially if they are piled up. Should they fall over, they could break the tank or even kill the occupants.

Never forget that rodents in general love to gnaw and will 'work away' at anything. Make sure that anything made of plastic is out of their reach. Tiny splinters of plastic may be swallowed and could damage the gut of these little creatures.

Giving these animals material to satisfy their urge for gnawing will be discussed later (see below and p. 30).

Opposite: *The exercise wheel is only really fun with two. Oil the axle of the wheel with salad oil or butter occasionally.*

A home for mice or rats

- **Wood shavings** can be used as litter. As mentioned above, they are absorbent, hygienic and cheap to buy. Rats and mice dig less frequently than gerbils and a layer 2–4 cm (³/₄–1¹/₂ in) thick will be sufficient.
- It is a good idea to add a layer of very absorbent **cat litter** wherever the animals regularly urinate, usually in corners. This will also help to bind the odours. Rats and mice, particularly males, will create far more odour than gerbils.
- Upside-down clay **flowerpots** with a suitable entry point make suitable sleeping-quarters for rats and mice. Rats do not gnaw nearly as much as gerbils, so small **nesting boxes** made of wood (with or without a floor) are recommended, although these may become smelly after a time. Experience has shown that rats prefer smaller sleeping-quarters to larger ones. Recommended dimensions (length × width × height) are about 18 × 15 × 13 cm (7 × 6 × 5 in) and the box should have a removable lid and an entry, about 5–6 cm (2–2¹/₂ in) in diameter, at the side.
- Cardboard or paper **cartons** provide **gnawing facilities** as well as shelters. Naturally, only use clean material. Shredded **paper bedding** can be offered as nesting material.

Small ladders are easy to attach to the sides of cages with bars.

Exercise wheels and climbing facilities

The hamster **exercise wheels** offered in pet-stores are very suitable for mice, rats and gerbils. It is essential to use only fully enclosed wheels for these rodents. The tails of gerbils especially are very easily damaged and may be injured if they become caught in an open-mesh wheel. Exercise wheels can be either free-standing or attached to the bars of the cage. Free-standing metal wheels that can be 'oiled' with salad oil or butter should be used in glass tanks. Plastic wheels are quieter but can be gnawed to pieces. An exercise wheel for rats needs to be much larger but, as rats tend to be less interested in using them, it is not absolutely necessary to offer one.

If you are good at simple carpentry, you could offer your mice and rats a raised **plank**, on a secure base, which they can sit on. This is easy to install in a cage with bars. The plank must be removable so that it can be cleaned periodically. In glass tanks, set up small **ladders** so that the animals can explore at various levels. A few small **branches** from a birch tree, beech tree or hazel bush should be added for your pets to nibble or climb on. Make sure you use only twigs and branches that are guaranteed to be free of traffic fumes, pesticides or other environmental pollution because rodents are sensitive to contamination.

There is plenty of room for two adventurous mice both on top of this coconut shell and inside it.

When equipping a glass tank or cage, make sure that cleaning the container will be an easy task to carry out. A dirty, smelly container will soon mar your enjoyment of its inhabitants and is likely to ruin their health.

Food- and water-containers

Use only firm-standing ceramic or pottery containers for food. Plastic containers will sooner or later be damaged by gnawing. To prevent food-containers becoming covered in litter stand them on a small wooden base or on a flat stone.

Drinking-water for rodents should only be provided in **drinking-bottles.** Open water-containers will soon become dirty or be buried by the animals and the litter will become damp.

Drinking-bottles with stainless steel spouts can be fixed onto the cage from the outside and at the correct height for the animals. In glass tanks, fix them to the side of the tank with suction pads or the special attachments sold in pet-stores. Another option is to use drinking-bottles that can be suspended from the bars with a piece of wire or a special fitment.

Choosing and buying a mouse, rat or gerbil

Rats and mice, like gerbils, are usually available from most **pet-stores.**

Another way of acquiring the rodents of your choice is to study the small advertisements in **specialist magazines**. In these publications, breeders offer their animals for sale. This is probably the best route if you are seeking a particular colour variety or show stock.

Nevertheless it is still advisable to select your own animals. Alternatively, if you can find the address of a specialist-club secretary, he or she may be able to put you in touch with a local **breeder**.

As can be seen, these mice seem to be particularly at home in this little house; they are able to watch everything going on but can also hide away in a flash.

How to recognize a healthy rodent

- The animals should be neither sitting apathetically on the ground nor running about frantically in their cage. It is also important to check whether they are already used to spacious, clean containers. Animals which are being kept in stuffy, dirty containers should be avoided as they are more likely to fall ill after the stress of the move.
- The **fur** should be shiny and not display any bald spots. Loss of hair may be caused by a variety of different factors (see p. 45) and is very difficult to treat and cure. A lengthy treatment will often make it hard to gain the animal's trust. On the other hand, small scars (e.g. on the tail or ears) need not be a sign of illness

17

Curious mouse with apple.

but are probably left-over from previous fights and bites.

- The **eyes** should be bright and shiny, with no evidence of tear-staining.
- The **anus** and the area around it should on no account be dirty. This is symptomatic of diarrhoea, which will often quickly lead to death.
- Animals that are conspicuously **thin** but otherwise appear healthy are usually quite old. An animal whose spine can be seen through its fur, or which has a crooked back, should not be bought – even if you are sorry for it. Such a purchase would benefit only the vendor and not help the old or sick animal.

One rodent or several?

Gerbils should never be kept as solitary individuals because they are highly sociable by nature and therefore need the company of other gerbils as much as they need food. They are naturally trustful and do not need to be tamed so simply keeping them alone will not make them any tamer.

If you have a large enough glass tank at your disposal, you will be able to keep a pair and allow one or two litters of young to remain with the parents. Under these conditions such a group will not produce any more young because of a natural regulatory mechanism. In this way a stable, mixed-sex family group can be maintained for years. On the other hand, it may be better to set up a single-sex group from the outset, to avoid any problems with young stock.

What could this little box be for? Even the mouse's tail seems to be forming a question mark. Mice prefer to hide away rather than be trapped in the open.

If you wish to keep a **mouse** or **rat** as a solitary individual, you should consider the following points:

- Will you have enough time each day, mainly in the evening, to spend with this new member of your household?
- The mouse or rat may climb up your body or slip beneath your clothing to satisfy its need for warmth and closeness to its owner, and for a feeling of security in dark, sheltered conditions.

If you are willing to accept this kind of behaviour, the animal will develop extraordinary devotion to you, its owner, as well as a high capacity for learning.

Nevertheless, it is much more natural to keep two or more animals together,

although you will need to offer them a much larger cage to make them feel comfortable. Rats and mice should not be kept in the same cage because they will not get on well together.

From carefully monitored experience, I can recommend keeping one rat on its own to begin with so that the animal can adjust better to its owner. After a few weeks, the second animal can be introduced. It will be less tame but will serve as a social and play partner for the first.

There is a risk of fighting when bringing together two animals that do not know each other, so this should only be done on neutral ground, i.e. outside the familiar cage and under strict supervision. Often, a completely rearranged, cleaned and 'deodorized' cage will distract the original animal and make it more likely to accept its new partner.

Mice as trapeze artists. Skilfully and surely, they walk along this rope, with their tails always serving as a balance and an 'emergency anchor' in tricky situations.

A young rodent or an older one?

In view of the fairly short life expectancy of rodents, it is advisable to purchase only young animals. Young rodents can be taken from their mother without harm at about 4 weeks after birth.

A male rodent or a female?

- In female rodents the distance between the anus and the genital opening is much smaller than in males.
- In male rodents the paired testicles – which are usually fairly obvious, even in quite young animals – are visible at the base of the tail and can be felt with the fingers. The gap between the anus and the genital opening is clearly greater than in females.

Note that the sexual differences are often more visible in naked, new-born young than in young with fur. Even in these tiny rodent babies, the gap between the anus and the genital opening can be seen quite clearly. The females also have two rows of clearly visible, tiny teats along their bellies (see illustrations, left).

The question of the rodents' sex only becomes important if you definitely wish to breed from a pair, or, conversely, do not want any offspring. Two males or two females will, as a rule, get on well together, particularly if they are from the same litter or were put together as half-grown youngsters. Male mice and rats have the disadvantage of emitting a more powerful smell than the females. They may, however, live a little longer.

In the case of gerbils, you should either take animals from just one family group or put together 4- to 6-week-old youngsters. If you leave it any later it will be almost impossible for these animals to get accustomed to each other because they tend to become fixated on their group's odour.

The odour of their own social group is the most important means of recognition among all rodents. The odour will change according to their surroundings. This is why animals which once lived together, or came from the same litter, lose this ability to recognize each other later on. Visual recognition plays a much smaller part in these odour-oriented creatures than it does in higher mammals, including human beings.

Transporting your rodents home safely

Plastic (acrylic) containers with a barred cover and one or two handles, as sold in pet-stores, are very suitable for transporting rats and mice. These carrying containers come in various sizes and

Top: *The distance between the anus and the genital opening in a female is quite small.* Bottom: *In males, the distance between the two openings is visibly greater.*

A practical ventilated carrying container for mice, also useful as a temporary home when you are cleaning out their quarters.

colours. If you purchase a slightly larger carrier, you can use it as a small spare cage when cleaning the main cage and as temporary accommodation for young animals.

In order to prevent the animals slipping about in these containers and harming themselves, put in plenty of wood shavings and hay. It is not necessary to provide food during the journey. The stress created during the move means that they will stop eating anyway. While travelling, the animals will feel more secure if the carrier is kept dark. It goes without saying that the carrier should be protected from exposure to extreme weather conditions. In a car, rodents should not be subjected to high temperatures and they should never be placed in the boot (trunk), because they might be poisoned by exhaust fumes.

If the journey to be taken is short (5–10 minutes), you can even use the **cardboard boxes** sold by pet-store-keepers. Experience has shown, however, that particularly keen gnawers can eat holes into such containers in a matter of minutes, and often start by enlarging the ventilation holes.

Be careful when picking up mice by their tail, e.g. to sex them. Provide adequate support and never leave them dangling in the air.

Adjustment period

Stress during the journey, and new smells, mean that most rodents will hide away when they first reach their new home. Gerbils, however, do not appear to be upset by anything and will usually be tame from the start.

New pets should be given plenty of time and patience. They should be allowed half a day, or even a whole day, of peace. It is, of course, understandable that you will be full of enthusiasm and curiosity during the first few days but this does not mean that you should invite all your friends and relatives to view the new member of the family immediately.

After spending a certain amount of time getting to know your pets, you can start to put your hand into the container, keeping it quite still and holding an item of food. After a while, the inquisitive little creatures will come out and sniff your hand, and nibble the titbit gently. You should not jerk away or you will destroy their newly acquired trust. Take care to ensure that the rodents do not bite your hand though. This will be painful and the wound is likely to bleed.

Taming your rodents

Mice grooming themselves in typical fashion.

The next thing your rodents will probably start to do is climb up your hand and you should keep it flat for this purpose. To mice and rats, human beings are just one huge climbing tree. Now you can try moving away from the cage, step by step, with the animal in your hand. Once this no longer frightens the rodent or makes it feel insecure, you will be almost there. The animal will trust you and you will have made a small friend which will be interested in you, even without the enticement of titbits, and which will feel just as secure with you as with the rest of its surroundings.

Unfortunately, there are always particularly stubborn individuals which do not respond, even after weeks of patient overtures. Usually, it is an older animal – one that has been kept on their own and given no attention when young – which reject all attempts at getting closer to it. In this case, the only other options are to try to entice the nervous animal with titbits or to provide it, very cautiously, with a partner of the same sex.

In extreme cases, you can remove the animal, however unwilling, from its hiding place and put it under your shirt or sweater. The comfortable body warmth and darkness in this 'human hiding place' may help it to 'thaw out', although, if frightened, your pet may bite you.

Mutual trust between animals and human beings living together is always very important. The owner must trust the animal and, vice versa, the animal must be able to trust the owner. A certain degree

This is the easy way to pick up a mouse or rat by its tail. Gerbils have a thinner skin on their tail which may tear under stress, especially at the tip. If this happens the skin of the tail could separate from the bone.

of tameness is therefore needed for the benefit of both parties. You will derive little enjoyment from a rodent that, on perceiving a human being, either freezes or whisks away into a hiding place. This will definitely be the reaction of wild animals but even animals kept in captivity will occasionally behave in this way.

How to handle your rodents

Most small mammals have enemies, e.g. owls or other predatory birds, that attack from above. Therefore it will take some time for a small rodent to learn that the hand which usually picks it up from above does not signify any danger. Allow it to sniff your hand, to give it confidence, rather than trying to pick it up straight away.

There are opposing views on the matter, but it is still better to restrain a mouse or rat by its tail until the animal has developed real trust.

Remember, though, that being grasped by its tail, while not painful, is still unpleasant for the animal. Hold the rat or mouse by its tail only briefly, grasping it at the base, near the body. Support the animal with your other hand so it is not left dangling by its tail. Gerbils should not be held in this way because their tails are easily damaged.

Tame mice, rats and gerbils like to have their back and the space between their ears gently rubbed or scratched with the fingertips. Mice and rats kept on their own really love this and will keep quite still, with half-closed eyes.

Tame, trusting animals will also not mind if you carefully lift them up by holding them beneath their belly. You can help mice to be less frightened of hands by making a small 'cave' with your two hands. A mouse will often voluntarily slip into this dark, warm shelter.

Should your rodents run free in a room?

In this situation, it would seem that the risks outweigh the benefits. Although such an expedition into a room will provide change for the animals, this apparent freedom has many inherent disadvantages. There is a risk of **other pets**, especially cats, getting into the room and catching the rodents.

Apart from this, the greatest dangers are probably those of **treading** on the little creatures or of them getting **jammed** between doors or windows. They may fall into and drown in open, **water-filled containers** or gnaw at **electric cables**. Only absolutely tame rats should be allowed out, but only under strict supervision. Such

rats may even respond to the sound of their own name – but you cannot call them back!

Gerbils and mice will often become so excited and upset by their new surroundings that they will try to hide in any nooks or crannies and squeeze between furniture.

You would not believe the many places into which mice choose to disappear: under and behind cupboards, boxes, bookshelves and free-standing furniture, and into upholstery. In a human dwelling place, a mouse that has been previously tame may become just as nervous and excitable, fast and elusive as its wild relatives.

Catching an animal that is so completely 'wound-up' entails considerable unnecessary stress for both the owner and the pet. For this reason, it is a much better idea to offer your mice, rats and gerbils variety and change inside their own cage and to take them out only for stroking and other displays of affection.

As mentioned above, tame rats are a possible exception because they respond with less fear to a new environment and may even display considerable curiosity in exploring and nibbling at everything new. You should, how- ever, never force a rat to run about in the room. During its main period of activity (usually dawn or dusk), simply place the cage or container on the floor, leaving the cage-door open

25

or removing the lid. To help the rat reach the floor, provide some sort of ladder or simply lean a rough length of wood against the container.

The rat will finally come out of its own accord and explore the room. The open cage-door will offer the animal a means of retreat and thus give it a feeling of security. Do not, however, lose sight of the rat. It is most important to disconnect any openly accessible electric cables and to remove any gnawable or delicate objects from the room. In any event, keep a close watch on your pet while it is loose in the room.

Pay particular attention to upholstery and fabric (especially curtains) as rats love to demolish these for nesting material. As soon as your pet begins to nibble at a 'forbidden' object, in spite of all your precautions, do not shout at it or punish it. Just remove the animal and give it something to nibble or gnaw.

A climbing tree

A good way of presenting your pets with some variety is to offer your own body as a 'climbing tree'. This activity is less suitable for gerbils because they are not particularly skilful at climbing and seem to have no head for heights.

What to do if your rodents escape

Should your pet manage to escape from its cage, because you have either forgotten to close the cage-door or not fixed the lid on properly, the first thing to do is to find out which room it is in. Traces of gnawing, as well as sounds of rustling, scratching, or even

A successfully tested mouse-trap: a cardboard tube with a little food in it!

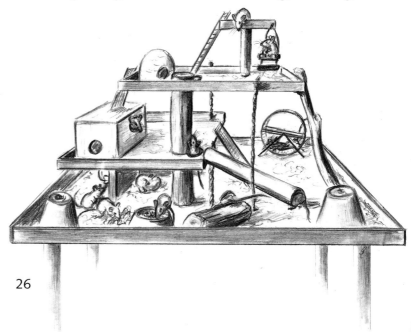

A multi-storey 'mouse-castle' on a table-top is a desirable and escape-proof living area for a mouse family, if covered with a suitable wire-mesh hood.

gnawing, especially after dusk, will indicate its whereabouts. Then place two or three **cardboard tubes**, each containing a little food, around the room.

After a while, the rodent will run inside one of these tubes to get at the food. Now, carefully and without frightening your pet, pick up the tube, closing both ends with your hands. You will then be able to put the rodent back into its cage with no problems.

If this method proves unsuccessful, place a tall **container**, filled with food and titbits as bait, in the room. Lean a small length of wood against the container to provide access. The rodent will smell the food, run up the 'ramp' and fall into the container.

This is probably a more successful version of the mouse-trap. Traps that do not harm rodents can be obtained from hardware stores and are another option. Fortunately, mice and gerbils are often, but not always, so dazed by their escape that they are quite easy to catch. Only after a period of freedom, the length of which depends on their individual natures, will they become 'wild' again and begin to hide or to react to a person's attempts at contact with hasty retreat and flight.

Above and below: As you can clearly see, a cardboard tube will be explored in detail without any qualms.

The right foods for your rodents

Mice and other rodents kept in captivity at home should be offered a varied, wide-ranging diet for their own good. In this way deficiency symptoms can be avoided. Left-overs from our own meals are harmful because these creatures cannot cope with salt and spices.

You should also not be indifferent to the health of these little animals by giving them old, rotten fruits and vegetables. When buying grain, make sure that it is fresh and that there are no webs from flour moths in the food. This can happen if the food has been stored in a bin for a long time.

Grain

The natural diet of all these rodents consists mainly of seeds. **Grain** contains a large proportion of carbohydrates and is therefore recommended as a staple food. Mouse **food mixture**, obtainable from pet-stores, is suitable but rather expensive. Hamster or guinea-pig food mixtures tend to be cheaper. Gerbils and mice should be given smaller seeds and grain as well. It is a good idea to mix in 20 per cent **budgerigar food** and about 10 per cent **canary seed**. Make sure that the guinea-pig food has no fatty components. Peanuts and sunflower seeds may be very popular with rodents but they are not particularly good for their figures!

Some pet-stores or pet-food retailers offer special **pressed food** or **pellets** for mice and rats. These are sold to many large-scale breeders, experimental laboratories and zoos. These pellets contain all the vital dietary ingredients except water, although rodents usually seem to prefer a more varied diet with a choice of different foodstuffs.

The staple grain diet can be supplemented with well-dried, hard, non-mouldy **bread**, **crispbread** and **oatflakes**. **Dog-flakes**, which contain added meat and vegetables are also an additional source of vitamins and protein.

Nibbling-sticks or cones offered in pet-stores are a good but relatively expensive source of food which will keep your rodents occupied.

Greenfood and softfood

A wide range of different kinds of **fruits** and **vegetables** will provide a ready supply of vitamins. The following are very suitable for both gerbils and mice: endive and 'Iceberg' lettuces, cucumber,

Opposite: *The old adage about catching mice with cheese still applies, as these five mice convincingly demonstrate. However, you should never offer large quantities to your pet.*

Above: *Nibbling-sticks are also very popular.*

Mice and rats, in particular, are specialists at being unspecialized and are fairly undemanding with food. In the wild, if there is a lack of food they will eat just about anything edible that they can get.

carrot, celery and beetroot, apples, hard pears, and berries, e.g. strawberries or raspberries, and grapes. Many small rodents cannot cope very well with very acidic fruits, e.g. oranges or kiwi fruit (Chinese gooseberries), so take care to give this type of food only in very small quantities.

Rats tend to be the less choosy and will eat all types of fruits and vegetables. Do not give flatulence-producing vegetables, e.g. cabbage and onions. Like human beings, rats love sweet things and bananas are particularly popular, although rather messy. Be prepared to wipe down the cage thoroughly because uneaten foods of this type will soon become mouldy.

Before giving any of these foods, wash them well with luke-warm water and dry them well.

Wafers are popular items for gnawing. Treats of this type are available from pet-stores.

Additional foods

In addition to the foodstuffs mentioned above, it is a good idea to offer **hay** regularly. This is particularly appreciated by gerbils. Hay is used for nest-building as well as food. Sprays of **millet**, as given to pet birds, are also always very welcome and all rodents like to spend time nibbling at them.

Opposite: Grain and seeds in a mixture with plenty of variety. Cereals, seeds, peanuts and sunflower seeds are a staple diet for mice but avoid offering too many oily seeds, e.g. sunflower, because of their relatively high fat content.

Branches of beech, birch, hazel or fruit trees are recommended as a food source and for gnawing and wearing down your rodents' teeth. You will see just how prized these 'nibbling-sticks from nature' can be. It goes without saying that they should be free from contamination by traffic fumes or pesticide sprays. If this is the case, the leaves can also be given as food.

An additional supply of protein can be very important. Give **dog-biscuits**, **dog-chews**, and **bones**, both as a source of protein and for gnawing. Small quantities of **sour cream**, **yoghurt** or mild hard **cheese** are always welcomed by mice and rats and are generally available in most households.

Pregnant and nursing females have higher protein requirements and should be supplied with a few **mealworm larvae** or a little hard-boiled **egg yolk**.

Vitamins and minerals

Vitamin supplements are unnecessary, provided that a very varied diet is supplied. Nevertheless, it is advisable to sprinkle a special small-animal vitamin supplement over the food every 2–3 days, keeping strictly to the recommended dosage on the packaging. The standard vitamin supplements intended for human beings should not be used because they are generally far too concentrated. An excess of vitamins can often be more harmful than a deficiency.

How much food will your rodents need?

The best approach is to give your rodents just sufficient food for a small amount to be left over the next day. (Always make sure that your pets do not hide food away or create stores.) This will also give you some idea of how much food they really need.

Like all living creatures, rodents show certain preferences and idiosyncrasies – certain individuals will enthusiastically consume a particular item of food that others will reject.

Drinking-water

There is no 'ideal' quantity of food, as demand for food will vary according to the age, size and individual traits of the animals. A sensibly devised menu with not too many fatty components will prevent your little pets from becoming fat.

A generous supply of softfood will help to meet the fluid requirements of gerbils, which tend not to drink large quantities of water. Even nursing rats could make do without a plentiful supply of water if they were to be given a great deal of fruit in their diet, although an adequate supply of water must be made available to them at all times.

Regular tasks

The main tasks that should be carried out each day are as follows:

- Remove spoiled softfood or greenfood that has been covered with wood shavings before the next feed.
- Feed your rodents, giving no more grain and greenfood than they require for the day.
- Replenish drinking-bottles, rinsing them out first.
- Check corners and hiding places in the cage where rodents may hide surplus food. If you find such food stores, remove them because many rodents have a habit of marking stores with urine. Moist seeds will quickly become mouldy.

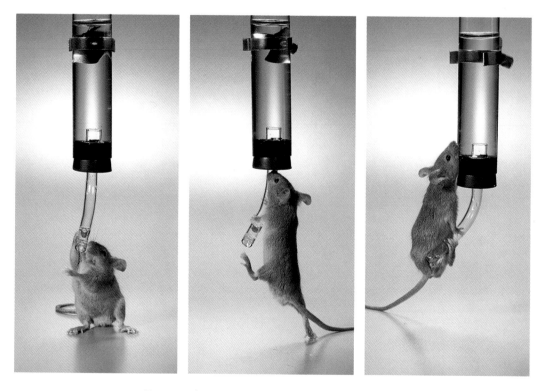

Mice will even seek to play with and explore their drinking-bottle. Note the attachment clip above. Some bottles can be suspended whereas others can be fitted through the sides of the cage.

Every 2 days:
- Remove areas of damp litter from corners where the rodents have urinated.
- Clean out drinking-bottles thoroughly with a bottle-brush, to prevent any build-up of algae.

About once a week:
- Give the entire cage a complete clean-out.
- Remove all the litter.
- Wash out the cage or glass tank with hot water and a safe disinfectant and, if necessary, wash off the sleeping-house and climbing facilities. Before returning the animals to their cage, let everything dry well and replace the litter.

The frequency of cleaning will depend on the size of the cage, the number of animals kept in it and the type of food they are given. A larger container need not be cleaned quite so often, provided that any damp litter and 'toilet' corners are cleaned out regularly.

Unfortunately, if cleaning is carried out too frequently it may result in disputes over hierarchy and increased territorial-marking behaviour. It is up to the owner to find the right balance. Gerbils produce a very concentrated urine in small volumes, so their cages generally need cleaning less often than those of rats or mice.

If there are a number of animals in one cage, and if they are given a generous diet of soft fruits, the cage will need to be cleaned more frequently. In any case, the penetrating smell, particularly of male mice and rats, will demand attention. Never use scented air-sprays or cleansers near the cage because they will harm the rodents' health.

Items given for gnawing should be renewed regularly as rodents lose interest in things that have been lying around in their cage for a long time.

Holiday time and domestic pets: making arrangements for small pets to be cared for in your absence is rarely as difficult or as costly as it is with dogs and cats.

Care during your holidays

Holidays and leisure periods usually cause nothing but stress and inconvenience for domestic pets. As a general rule, and only in extremely exceptional cases, a solitary mouse or rat that is accustomed to particularly close contact with its owner may be taken on holiday. If you are going abroad, you are unlikely to be able to take your pet because of quarantine regulations.

If you intend to take your pet with you, you should be absolutely certain that rodents will be accepted in your holiday quarters. If the journey there is only short and you intend to spend a long time at your destination, there is something to be said for taking your pet with you. Place it in a small, well-padded container for the journey. If possible, take its familiar cage as well. In spite of your closeness to your pet and affection for it, you should bear in mind that travelling represents a considerable risk for these animals. They could become sick in unfamiliar surroundings.

By far the best solution is to hand your rodents into the care of relatives, friends or rodent specialists near your home. These little pets are easy to look after and will not create a lot of work for their 'holiday carer'.

Gerbils at home.

Keeping your rodents occupied

If you keep a solitary mouse or rat as a pet, it is up to you to provide it with a substitute for the companionship of members of its own species. Needless to say, nothing a human being can do will be a complete substitute for the many activities undertaken by these animals in a small-group situation. Mutual grooming, licking, chasing or cuddling up together are simply a natural part of the daily life of these sociable creatures.

Regular stroking, gentle scratching or carrying the rodent around in your clothing will go some

way towards helping it to forget its lack of a partner. Allow your mouse or rat to explore your clothing from top to bottom; it is an ideal way of keeping it occupied.

Inside the cage, there are a number of ways to offer your pet variety. Cardboard packaging material, kitchen-tissue or toilet-paper tubes, as well as twigs and branches, will satisfy its urge to gnaw and provide it with something to do. You could also try hiding a few delicacies in a closed cardboard box, under some hay or in a screwed-up ball of paper. Your pet will then have to work for its food. Feeding it several times during the course of a day (fruit at one time, grain at another) will stimulate activity.

For mice, another option is a **mouse-castle**, often recommended as the sole accommodation. This several-storey, castle-like structure, which provides lots of hiding places for mice, should be placed on a free-standing surface, e.g. a table. As mice do not like jumping from great heights, they will usually not leave the table.

If you have the necessary skills, you can build an **automatic food-dispenser** for your rats that requires them to employ some effort and inventiveness to gain access to their food.

Gerbils are much easier to keep occupied as, in the wild, they live in an environment that hardly ever changes. Their main and apparently favourite activities are scratching, shovelling, digging and gnawing, but they become quite enthusiastic about change and variety.

Typical behavioural studies. The mouse below is heavily pregnant.

Breeding

As far as breeding is concerned gerbils are exceptional in the following way: if you allow a pair of gerbils to keep one or two of their litters, they will not produce any more offspring. This natural means of birth control is not found in mice or rats. However, if you remove the young, the parent gerbils, like other rodents, will become almost as fertile again. If you want to prevent your mice and rats producing offspring, use the only surest method: keep the sexes apart.

If you want to raise rodent offspring you should establish right from the start what you can do with all the young. Always count on large litters so that, later on, you do not find yourself left with too many animals.

An 11-month-old rat that I was given as a present, and which I expected to produce only a small litter because of her age, surprised me by producing 18 young, all of which she raised to adulthood. Her following litters were also large.

Finding good homes for even average-sized litters of six or

seven young mice can be a problem. You cannot count on pet-stores being interested and nor is an advertisement in a local newspaper certain to attract likely purchasers.

Mating and pregnancy

If you wish to watch the reproductive behaviour and rearing of young just once, the best idea is to put together just one pair of rodents. There should be no problems with fighting because the sexual urge is generally stronger than the urge to reject an animal that is not a member of the same social group.

It is best to put the female into the male's cage for pairing, or to allow mating to take place on 'neutral territory'. Females will mate again almost immediately after giving birth, which means that they will shortly produce another litter. Male rats and mice make peaceable fathers, some of them even helping with the care of the young.

Mice become sexually mature at an age of 30–49 days, rats at 30–70 days and gerbils at 60–80 days. They do not attain their fully grown state until much later, often after 6 months of age.

At the approach of a male, a fertile female who is ready to mate will adopt a hollow-backed position and lay her tail to one side. Copulation will last only a few seconds, after which both partners will lick each other's genitals.

During the period of willingness to mate (oestrus), copulation will take place several times. During the 20- to 24-day gestation period the female will start to have a higher requirement for food and fluids and this will last throughout the rearing period. She should be given a protein-rich diet during this time.

About a week before the birth, the pregnant rodent will spend time collecting nesting material and padding the sleeping-quarters for her offspring. A few days before the birth she will no longer tolerate the male around the area of the nest.

Baby mice are carried in the mother's mouth.

Birth and nursing

The birth generally takes place in the early hours of the morning. Provided that the animals with which you are dealing have no behavioural problems and are not very shy, the young will be produced in quick succession and will be immediately suckled.

During the nursing period, which lasts approximately 3 weeks (almost the same for mice, rats and gerbils), the animals should be looked after diligently. In the case of shy animals, even if the necessary quiet and care are

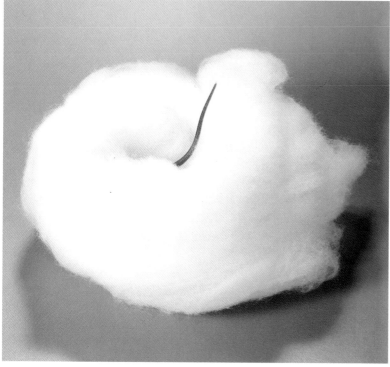

This special nesting cotton can be used to build caves and passages. Finally, all that is visible is a mouse tail. Care is needed if the mice get their claws caught in it.

New-born mice in a nest.

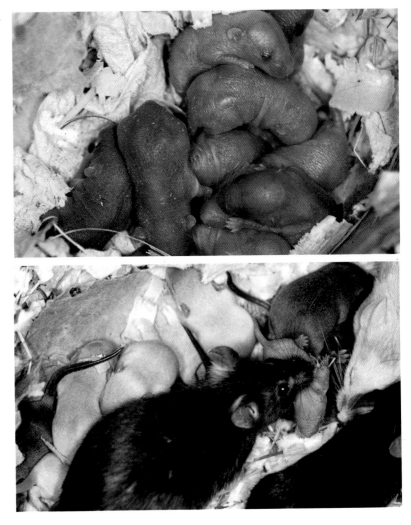

A communal nest belonging to several females with young of different ages.

given, it may easily happen that the young are either eaten by the mother immediately after their birth or neglected.

This type of behaviour can create disgust in human beings but there is a very natural reason for it. In an environment that is too unsafe or uncertain for offspring, it makes more sense for the adult to reabsorb the nutrients which she has expended (i.e. the young) and to breed again later at a more favourable time. You should therefore avoid any interference unless you suspect that something is wrong.

Only very tame and trusting animals will tolerate a human hand near the nest. For this reason, be careful as many animals that are perfectly tame under normal circumstances will react aggressively during the nursing period.

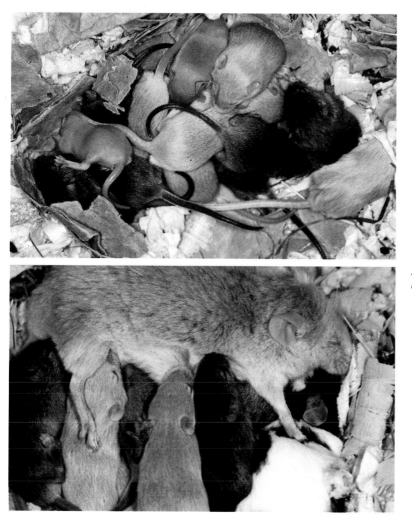

10- to 14-day-old mice.

A self silver mouse nursing its babies.

About 3 weeks after the birth, you may carefully attempt to pick up the young in your hand. At 4 weeks of age, the young animals are quite independent and can then be separated from their mother.

Development of the young

New-born mice, rats and gerbils are typically naked, blind and deaf. The only point of reference to which they are geared to respond is the mother's 'milk-bar'.

A few days after the birth, you will be able to see the first sign of hair around the head. After about 2 weeks, the eyes of the young rodents will be open and the little ones will begin actively to explore their surroundings. Babies that manage to crawl out of the nest will be carried straight back by their mother with great alacrity. At this age, even the tiniest gaps will present no barrier, so be sure that the bars of the cage are not too widely spaced. The youngsters will also rapidly become acquainted with adult food during their first explorations. About 3 weeks after their birth – a little later for large litters – the youngsters will become independent of their mother's milk.

If the female does not immediately produce a further litter, allow the youngsters to stay with their mother for another week or two. During this time, they will become familiar with the group's social activities and learn to recognize dangers.

In the case of these sociable rodents, there are usually no problems if the youngsters remain with the group and the mother produces another litter. The female will accept them all, even though the older ones will attempt to crowd out the new-born babies in order to get at their mother's milk again. For this reason, it is better not to allow females to mate again immediately after giving birth, as long as they do not appear to object. Gerbils are an exception in this respect. A pair should not be split up because bringing them together again later would probably end in fights and biting.

Colour varieties of mice, rats and gerbils

Mice come in a wide variety of different colours. These include:

- **Agouti** – the natural wild colour, similar to that of the wild house mouse.
- **Self (pure)** – such as **black**, which must show no trace of other colour, e.g. odd white hairs, in their coat. The **self silver** is a light grey colour and **self blue** is a dark smoky grey. The **self red** is anther popular variety in this group.
- **Tans** –resembling self varieties but with tan underparts. The depth of the tan coloration varies according to the variety.
- **White** – usually albino with typically red eyes; a separate variety has black eyes.
- **Himalayan** – a particularly attractive patterned variety, the extremities being dark brown in colour and offset against the pure white body coloration. These markings closely resemble those of the Siamese cat.
- **Patched** – in various different colours, with varying dark and light areas of fur.

42

Breeding colour varieties of mice requires a lot of time and effort – and a lot of space. It is almost impossible to avoid the formation of odours, so a well-ventilated room will definitely be needed to house the mice. Because of the quick succession of generations, results can be obtained in a very short time.

Breeding for colour requires a basic knowledge of Mendel's laws, the laws of biological inheritance. You will find details of these in most biology books or specialist literature. They apply to all living creatures and can easily be applied to a breeding colony of mice, as well as rats and gerbils.

Rats come in fewer colour varieties than mice. These are:

- **Natural** wild colour – called **'agouti'**, although this is a browner hue, and widely available.
- **Albino** – one of the commonest colour varieties.
- **Self (pure)** – such as **black**, which is also very frequently available. In my experience, black rats are the more popular as they do not have the red eyes of albinos, which somehow always look unhealthy. The **cream**, often with red eyes, is more difficult to obtain. Other self varieties include the **self chocolate** and the **dilute**, called the **self mink**, which is coffee coloured.
- **Patched** – the most common colour variety. Hooded rats are a widely kept patterned form, with a white body and a coloured head, the darker areas here extending down the back.

Gerbils are generally available in the following colour varieties:

- **Natural** wild colour – the original grey-brown colour with pale underparts that provides the best form of camouflage in the steppes of Mongolia. It is sometimes described as **'agouti'**.
- **Black** – very often available, frequently with white patches.
- **Argente** – a golden shade with a pure white belly.
- **White** – either pure albino or sometimes with a dark tip to the tail. All have pink eyes.
- **Cream** – an off-white colour bred from a combination of the argente and pink-eyed white.
- **Patched** – usually asymmetrically distributed patches of colour; only recently available on the market.

Fur types of mice and rats

- **Long-haired** mice and rats, like angora cats, have longer fur than normal.
- The **satin** factor produces conspicuously shiny fur but, at present, occurs only in mice.
- **Rex** varieties have a slightly curled coat and curly whiskers.

The sick rodent

If they are kept in clean surroundings and generally well cared for your pets should not suffer greatly from illness. When a pet does fall ill rapid veterinary attention should lead to its recovery. As a rule, always ask a veterinarian or other expert for advice if you suspect symptoms of disease, as the risk of making the wrong diagnosis or of harming the animal by giving the wrong medication is considerable.

Parasites

Although rodents are known to be carriers of disease and hosts of parasites, those bred under human supervision experience surprisingly few problems in this respect. A veterinarian will be able to advise you on the best treatment for a parasitic problem.

Symptoms of illness: a lethargic and apathetic mouse with fluffed-up fur.

Mites and **lice** can both cause hair loss and severe itching patches with crusty-looking skin. Mites can only be identified under a microscope. Lice are usually introduced by animals obtained from stock that has not been looked after properly.

Fleas are very unusual in pet rodents and will only really bother the animal if the infestation is severe.

Intestinal parasites, such as **worms**, can only be positively identified from specimens of droppings. A severe infestation will gradually lead to weight loss, even though the animal eats normally. Worms are usually acquired via soil or contaminated food. Various different preparations are very effective for such problems but the correct dosage must be adhered to. Infections of **single-celled organisms** (protozoans) may cause diarrhoea.

Common ailments

Small wounds from bites and **injuries** usually heal up very quickly and without any problems. Disinfecting or treating injuries in rodents rarely accelerates the normal course of healing. Only if the animal's movements are visibly impaired should a veterinarian be consulted.

Swellings or **ulcers** that are clearly visible may arise on different parts of the body. If these enlarge very rapidly, and feel slightly hot to the touch, they may be pus-filled **abscesses** which are often the results of bites. These will usually burst open by themselves after a while. Bathing with salt water may bring the abscess to a head, allowing the pus to drain out. In older rats and mice, swellings are indicative of **cancer**. Let your veterinarian decide whether an operation would be sensible or successful but, at all costs, avoid letting your pet suffer.

Diarrhoea is indicated by soft, smeary faeces and may be due to any of several causes, such as infection with bacteria, viruses or single-celled organisms (protozoans). This usually only occurs if the animal has been additionally weakened by living in unsuitable conditions. Spoiled food, unclean litter and pests will also lower its resistance.

As soon as diarrhoea occurs cut out, greenfood or softfood. If this does not improve matters, consult a veterinarian without delay as quick treatment gives the best chance of recovery.

Respiratory infections are indicated by clearly audible breathing, frequent sneezing and slightly sticky eyes. Possible triggers are dampness in the cage, draughts or sudden fluctuations in temperature. Eliminate the causes and position the cage where it can be kept at a temperature of about 22–23°C (72–73°F). Additional doses of vitamin supplements (those designed for animals) may help to boost the immune system. If only one animal in the group is affected, it should be isolated

Many respiratory illnesses among rodents are extremely infectious. If there is no rapid recovery, take the rodent to an experienced veterinarian and have it examined thoroughly. Many illnesses that seem harmless may be caused by viruses or bacteria and these are very difficult to treat, even with medication.

Accidental injuries may occur, particularly if your pet falls to the ground from a great height, when it may remain lying on the ground as if dead. Very often it will have gone into **shock**. Lay the animal carefully back in its cage and keep it warm. Watch it closely. If it has not sustained **internal injuries** it will soon start moving again. Abnormal movements, such as dragging of a limb, may indicate an injury. You should then take it to a veterinarian.

Dental problems may arise, particularly if the incisor teeth, which are used for gnawing and continue to grow throughout the rodent's life, are not being worn down adequately. Prevent these kind of problems by providing your rodents with sufficient opportunities to wear down their teeth on branches or dried crusts of bread. These problems may also be due to a deformation of the jaw, caused by an injury or a congenital defect. Unfortunately there is no cure for this. Either the teeth will have to be trimmed constantly or the animal will have to be put down. Affected animals should never be used for breeding purposes.

Old age is often manifested by loss of weight and dull fur. Rodents may become less active, their fur may lose its shine and become thinner, and they lose weight, despite adequate food.

Index

Picture sources
All the photographs are by Regina Kuhn, of Stuttgart, except for those on pages 40 and 41, which are by Andreas Boisits. All black-and-white illustrations are by Siegfried Lokau of Bochum-Wattensschied.

Acknowledgements
My thanks go to my brother Michi, my parents, Andreas, Anja, Gernot, Gudrun, Ulli and especially to Birgit Gollmann and my brother Frank for all their help.

A BLANDFORD BOOK
First published in the UK 1997 by Blandford
A Cassell imprint
Cassell plc
Wellington House 125 Strand London WC2R 0BB

Text copyright © 1997 Cassell plc
Translated by Astrid Mick
Originally published as *Mäuse* by Georg Gassner
World copyright © Eugen Ulmer GmbH & Co., Stuttgart, Germany

Distributed in the United States by Sterling Publishing Co., Inc., 387 Park Avenue South, New York, NY 10016-8810

A Cataloguing-in-Publication Data entry for this title is available from the British Library

ISBN 0-7137-2679-2

Printed and bound in Spain